ELLE DECOR
PORTFOLIOS

BEDROOMS

Cover: photo © Alexandre Bailhache
Reportage Marie Kalt

Copyright © 2003 Filipacchi Publishing for the present edition
Copyright © 2001 Editions Filipacchi, Société SONODIP – *Elle Décoration*, for the French edition

Translated from French by Simon Pleasance and Fronza Woods
Copy edited by Matthew J.X. Malady

ISBN: 2 85018 613 9

Color separation: Hafiba

Printed and bound in Italy by Canale

BEDROOMS

filipacchi
publishing

We leave it in the morning, nostalgically. And return to it at night, happily. We spend almost half our lives in it. So it is absolutely fundamental to feel good in this place that belongs only to us. The bedroom is the most private room in the house—the place that speaks volumes about our tastes and our personalities, sometimes in spite of ourselves. When it comes to decorating the bedroom, we give free rein to our desires and imaginations, try to stamp "our" bedroom with the hallmarks of our lives.

But the bedroom is also a shrine to idleness. In it, nothing is spared when it comes to creature comforts. The bed, needless to say, is the centerpiece. Whether wedged beneath an attic roof or nestled in an alcove, the bed is the key element of a bedroom's decoration. And on this palette, a range of headboards competes with the many kinds of canopies and four-posters of yesteryear, brought back into fashion by inspired designers.

When size permits, bedrooms can be turned into living rooms, no less. Some people even set up their office in them, or create a space for a small library. Others make room for bathtub and sink.

In the following pages, we invite you to draw inspiration from the ideas of great interior designers, and adopt tricks and eccentricities from ordinary individuals who have shown an extraordinary passion for decoration.

CONTENTS

BEDROOMS
FOR LIVING IN

BEDROOMS FOR LIVING IN ARE MUCH MORE THAN ORDINARY BED-ROOMS. SURROUNDING THE BED MAY BE A LIBRARY OR AN OFFICE. BEDROOMS ARE THUS TRANSFORMED INTO ROOMS THAT ARE NICE TO LIVE IN EVERY MOMENT OF THE DAY.

Left. In this erstwhile studio in the heart of Paris, antique dealer Christian Sapet has created an intimate and eclectic setting, with books here, there and everywhere. The library consists of evenly spaced rough planks filling the wall from floor to ceiling.
Above. To make the bedroom appear bigger, Sapet installed two sliding mirrors, which cunningly lengthen the bookshelves and hide a dressing room beyond.

Above. The bedroom in this London apartment —which was revamped by interior designers David Champion and Anthony Collett, who also designed much of the furniture—displays a strong personality. The cushions match the 17th century carpet and pick out the blue of the Chinese vases placed atop a wardrobe designed to hide hi-fi equipment. The curtains are of silk taffeta, and the cream hues are well matched to the soft range of blues.

Above. For this New Jersey collector with a passion for windvanes and weathercocks, decorator Brigitte Semtob created a space where the emphasis is on airiness and the outdoors. This is a bedroom with clean lines, where the harmony comes mainly from the choice of delicate, complementary colors. The glass roof, like the side windows, makes the room very light. The furniture is of Canadian beech. Above the bed rests a statue of a horse, and to its left a 19th century copper centaur.

BEDROOMS
FOR LIVING IN

For the owners of this
apartment in the Left Bank
of Paris, decorator
Brigitte Semtob has chosen
sober colors so as to highlight
their art collection.
In the bedroom, the sheets
trimmed with red braid and
the cashmere bedspread add
a bright, dynamic touch,
breaking away from the
overall bluish feel. The relief
on board hung over the bed,
as well as the "Red Circle"
rug, are by Jean Arp.

Above. A harmony of camel-colored hues for this bedroom, with furniture designed by Frédéric Méchiche. The purity of the lines used in this resolutely contemporary style go perfectly with the comfort and warmth of the cashmere and the checkerboard oak paneling. The result is a luminous atmosphere that enhances the art collected by the owners—like this Keith Haring triptych, with its crisp graphic effects. The bedside lamps are by Ingo Maurer.

Above. With this bedroom, East meets West on the shores of the Bosphorus. Mehmet Bay and Zeynep Garan went to Anouska Hempel for their Istanbul home, and she designed its volumes. The decorator opted for a play of black and ginger hues, and this combination permits pleasant contrasts with the white and rust-colored stripes. The lacquered 16th century furniture and the windows, with their Japanese blinds, are all Oriental in inspiration. Acting as headboards, old cherrywood and ebony doors are set against walls covered with tadlakt. On the window sill, a majestic ebony lamp and porphyry bowls.

BEDROOMS
FOR LIVING IN

A fantastic idea for a
book lover: to sleep
surrounded by the works
of his favorite authors.
Jacques Leguennec, an ardent
lover of literature, wanted
his bedroom to reflect his
passion and become part of
a library. He designed the room
himself, as he did the bookstore
lamps and the beech bedside
tables. In the alcove, clad in
white canvas, he has hung
an architectural drawing.

Above. This bedroom reflects the white magic of a duplex completely converted by Frédéric Méchiche, who also designed the furniture. The decoration is based on an outward simplicity: ivory-colored walls, bleached oak parquet flooring, armchairs swathed in white linen and cream canvas slipcovers on either side of French windows leading to a terrace that runs the length of the apartment. To add contrast, Méchiche implemented a halogen light and a granite and wrought iron table. All these features combine to create a calming, sophisticated setting.

Above. In this village house in the Ile de Ré, on France's Atlantic coast, a large bedroom with bathroom incorporated combines originality with ingeniousness. The pine-paneled walls have been impregnated with bondex, a kind of milk paint that stops the wood from darkening. In the alcove, the sink and bathtub have been set in the same wood so they blend in with the rest of the room. On the floor, made of rubbed terra cotta slabs, an English pine table is flanked by a pair of chairs covered in white piqué.

Left and above. Bill Blass was known to have asserted that color "distracts," which is why he used it with caution. Here, in his second home in New England, Blass played with somber, sober shades. The couturier's huge bedroom was a meeting room when this house was used previously as a tavern. The bed is covered in a patchwork quilt typical of New England. The staircase is not, as you might first think, a masterly work, but a surrealist sculpture. It is the only sign of fantasy amid a minimalist decoration that created a feeling of austere comfort. There are no curtains on the windows, but rather interior shutters.

Above. Decorator Michèle Halard, who designed this bedroom for her friends Jean-André and Geneviève Charrial, went after simplicity at all costs —be it in the colors or the floor coverings. As a result, the neutral tones accentuate the brightness and beauty of the raspberry-hued curtains, sheets and painted wooden shelves which are fitted to masonry uprights. The zinc lamp and the rug were designed by Yves Halard.

Above. This apartment in New York's Greenwich Village shows the practical spirit of a small bedroom organized around the bed, making it possible to get the most out of the available space. The charm of the open brickwork of the fireplace, together with the gold-colored woodwork is emphasized by the window, which floods the room with light. On either side of the fireplace, storage units combine bookshelves with drawer space. The bed stands on a North Carolina pine floor. A potentially cramped room that has been most cunningly done up.

In decorating the Provençal
farmhouse of her friend Sarah
Saint-George, Maxime de la
Falaise has mixed styles and
colors together with great
panache. The "portraits
bedroom," shows the daring
of a reined-in free spirit,
improvising around Polish and
Oriental themes. There is a lot
of imagination and originality
in the combination of different
prints—particularly for the
canopied bed, embellished with
embroidered fabrics and exotic
silks. But the most striking
feature is the use made of color.
Maxime has painted the walls
with colored distempers in
ocher and pistachio. The paint
was applied first with a brush,
then spread with a cloth.
Beyond the Moroccan rug,
two portraits of Maxime by
her father, Sir Oswald Birley,
frame the fireplace.

BEDROOMS
FOR LIVING IN

In the bedroom of his Seattle
duplex, which opens onto a
huge terrace, Terry Hunziker
favors gray and honey hues,
creating a thoroughly soft-
edged modernity. The decorator
has used a wide range of
materials. The walls are thus
covered with Venetian plaster—
a kind of tadlakt—while the
floor is covered with sisal.
The bed, chaise longue, chair
and occasional table were
all designed by Terry. The wall
light over the bedside table
was made by Miguel Milla.
The end wall is covered with
photos by Irving Penn, Paul
Blanca, Martin Chambi and
Michael Kenna. The end
result is an atmosphere at
once contemporary and warm.

BEDROOMS FOR LIVING IN

Above. This Provençal farmhouse, decorated by Jacques Grange for his friends Terry and Jean de Gunzburg, displays a wealth of details and patterns in a vast bedroom. Here we can clearly see the structure of the "bedroom-study-loggia-winter living room" for which he drew up the plans. Framing the bed are lamps and bedside tables by Vincent Corbière. On the right, there is a drawing by Wendy Artin and a 19th century Basque gourd. At the foot of the bed, which was designed by Vincent Corbière, is a sculpture by a young Spanish artist, "Yaguès," set on an Ethiopian mat. Precious decorative objects hailing from all over the world abound in this room, which places great emphasis on straight lines and right angles.

Above. Here we see the bedroom from another angle, showing the living room area. The sculpture wall made of "cocciopesto"—a mixture of egg shells and terra cotta—was designed by Jacques Grange for the Galerie Farnese. The oak and leather furniture is by Royère, and the pair of iron and leather armchairs were created by Giacometti for Jean-Michel Frank. The rug is by Georges Braque. On the upper, separating wall, reside frieze-like photos of Marilyn Monroe by Bert Stern.

BEDROOMS
FOR LIVING IN

In Normandy, we find an
erstwhile staging-post converted
by Julie Prisca. In the bedroom-
cum-bathroom, with furniture
designed by the decorator
and her son, gentle colors reign,
and add tasteful bareness to
the room. The lilac walls and
Julie Prisca's mauve and brown
bed linen complement one
another beautifully. The room
reflects a subtle compromise,
combining rustic charm and
urban modernism.

ATTIC
BEDROOMS

SIMPLE PLEASURE: SLEEPING RIGHT UNDER THE ROOF... BY PLACING GREAT IMPORTANCE ON NATURAL MATERIALS, ATTIC BEDROOMS GO FOR AUTHENTICITY. THE BEAMS AND OPEN STONEWORK WHICH THEY PROUDLY DISPLAY LEND THEM A WARM, RUSTIC CHARM.

Left. This bedroom, in designer Julie Prisca's Normandy home, displays simplicity full of charm. The mix of painted woodwork, the quilted bedspread and tulle creates a very gentle atmosphere.

Above. A Baroque touch for this Provence bedroom designed with African hues by Maxime de la Falaise for her friend Sarah Saint-George.

Left. In her manor house in the middle of the English countryside, Lady Weinberg has installed this bed—which she has designed like a bunk in a boat—in the garret. On the wall, broad bands of whitewash match the parquet flooring. On the left, a 19th century farmhouse chair in bleached oak.

Right. At Porquerolles, off France's Mediterranean coast, this bedroom in the attic reflects a tranquil modernity with its intentionally spare decoration. Its contrasting shades of color and the presence throughout of wood—here worked by Daniel and Olivier Pelenc—add a warm touch. The wall lights, seed merchant's furniture and armchairs call a certain colonial style to mind.

ATTIC BEDROOMS

Comfort and romanticism are
on exhibit in François d'Armor's
bedroom in the Bagnols Castle
hotel, located in the Beaujolais
region of France. Beneath the
original timberwork and beams,
the four-poster beds have been
trimmed with old toile de Jouy.
The club chairs have been
re-covered with linen slipcovers.
An authenticity created by
using of darkish wood,
lends a rustic allure to
this huge bedroom.

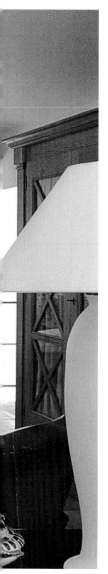

Left. The interior of this farmhouse—which rests at the foot of the Luberon range in southern France—combines Indonesian furniture and warm hues to create a decoration akin to the colonial style. The owners, Michèle and Paul Belaiche, were keen to have a bedroom that is perfect for living in. The floor, made of terra cotta tiles, is covered with rattan mats from Borneo. The low, bamboo table is from Java. The settee, buried beneath patterned cushions, comes from Indonesia. The leather armchairs are from the 1930s.

Right. This home of a Belgian collector illustrates a successful mix of genres expressing ethnic influences. A boxed-in area serves as both a headboard and a shelf for a collection of traditional objects, photos and a Russian Cubist painting. At the foot of the bed, art books are laid out on an Indonesian table. In the foreground, on the left, a Dogon ladder frames the room.

39

ATTIC BEDROOMS

Left. This Harbour Island house in the Bahamas belongs to a person with a passion for architecture and decoration. This house, like a boat, was built entirely of timber. For the bedroom, the bed, which is based on an Indian model, was built on the spot. The patchwork bedspread and the collection of round boxes lend it a slightly "cottage-y" feel.

Right. A warm atmosphere abounds in the Boutchoux de Chavannes bedroom in the Bagnols Castle outbuildings. The room adopts a "country" style, at once simple and refined: The red-checked fabric surrounding the four-poster bed goes wonderfully well with the beams and open stonework.

ATTIC BEDROOMS

Left. A typically mountain ambience is presented in this bedroom at the Rosheim Hotel in Norway. It uses a chalet style, which puts great emphasis on painted and carved woodwork. The two beds are linked together by a desk, which has the same floral motif as the beds.

Right. An attic bedroom in the basement? This all-wood room adjoins the fitness room and sauna at the Albert I Hotel in Luxembourg. The two teak beds, with their original design inviting us to lie back and relax, were designed by architect Pia Muller.

Above. In this Provençal
farmhouse belonging to an
English family, interior
designers Anthony Collett
and Andrew Zarzycki opted
for the natural look. In the

children's bedroom,
the cladding is in painted
wood. Hazel wood has
been used for the bunk beds.
On the floor, there is a raffia
mat from Cogolin.

Above. This villa on the shores of lake Constance has been restored by Anthony Collett, John MacLeod and David Champion, who designed all the architectural features as well as the furniture. The attic bedroom is all softness and mellowness, with its white-painted, pine walls. A muslin veil has been draped around the corners of the iron four-poster bed, at the foot of which stand two Arts & Crafts stools. On the window seat and the armchair, ikats against a linen backdrop. The parquet floor is covered with a woolen carpet.

FOUR-POSTER BEDS
& CANOPIES

WITH THEIR ROMANTIC HANGINGS AND DRAPES, FOUR-POSTER BEDS
SEEM TO COME STRAIGHT OUT OF FAIRYTALES. DECORATOR ANOUSKA
HEMPEL IS ONE OF THE GREAT CANOPY SPECIALISTS. IN HER HOTELS,
SHE ARRANGES THESE BEDS IN A THOUSAND DIFFERENT WAYS.

Left. At Blakes Hotel in
Amsterdam, we find the
Anouska Hempel touch, with
the interplay of ginger and
charcoal gray stripes, in a
bedroom the color of wonderful
spices. On the walls, there is
a collection of perfectly
aligned mirrors. The window is
covered with bamboo blinds.

Above. Anouska Hempel
decorated the bedroom in a
villa near Palma de Majorca
in Spain. On the four-poster
bed—framed by linen curtains
acting as mosquito netting—
she has placed a mass of
straw cushions, in linen and
cotton. Syrian stools are
placed at the foot of the bed.

47

CANOPIES

Opposite. Karelia is the name of one of the six suites in the Hempel Hotel, the second hotel created by Anouska Hempel in London. What first strikes you about this room is its authentic design and its high-tech concept, influenced by the simplicity of the Orient. The four-poster bed is covered with linen and flanked by two screens. Beneath the bedside table, storage boxes in ecru fabric, which match the beige and white colors of the wood and fabrics. At the foot of the bed, a pair of Chinese "hunting chairs."

Right. Anouska Hempel has completely redesigned the architecture and arrangement of Blakes Hotel in Amsterdam —which was built in 1632, and formerly served as a theater. In this bedroom, with its raspberry and elephant hues— conjuring up military uniforms from colonial days—using lamps, tables and lacquered chests, the decorator plays with symmetrical effects.

CANOPIES

In Kensington, which is at
the heart of London,
Lady Weinberg has personally
seen to the decoration of the
52 bedrooms of Blakes Hotel.
She has used natural and
caramel color tones for this
light-filled suite, where
imaginative decor combines
with monastic rigor. The
furniture and fittings have been
unearthed from all over the
world. They add a personal and
sophisticated touch. The choice
of fabrics—white linen and raw
linen—gives the impression of
comfort, softness and well-being
which you only find at Blakes.

CANOPIES

Left. The bedroom in
this English manor house
at Cole Park, home of Lady
Weinberg, consists mainly
of objects brought back
from travels. The four-poster
bed features stone columns
imported from Rajasthan.
It is hung with linen curtains
made from old sheets, a
material also used for the
pillowcases and bedspread.
Two chairs from Pakistan sit
at the foot of the bed.

Right. Once again, a very
subtle interplay of stripes
by Anouska Hempel, in the
Jade suite at Blakes Hotel
in Amsterdam. For this
bedroom, which overlooks
the garden, Hempel used moss-
colored fabrics and paintwork.

CANOPIES

Left. A beige and white color scheme is used for this bedroom designed, once again, by Anouska Hempel, in a sumptuous holiday home. The harmony of the decor rests on the fine balance of the setting, the symmetry of the lines, and the way the cushions are set one atop the other. In the background, against the wall, resides a very beautiful Syrian chest of drawers made of inlaid mother-of-pearl.

Right. A stone's throw from the Trocadéro in Paris, behind a lovely dressed stone façade, stands Dokhan's Hotel. Interior decorator Frédéric Méchiche was keen to endow the hotel with the elegance and charm of a private home, and all the fabrics were made to his designs. In this luxurious suite, blue and white motifs are set off by the mahogany of the chairs. With its rotunda and bull's-eye window, the room is also distinctive for its architectural originality.

In the outbuildings of
Bagnols Castle, built
in the 13th century,
Paul and Helen Hamlyn
have designed eight
bedrooms with care and
attention to detail.
This one illustrates a
warm, rustic style,
with its topstitched English
bedspreads matching the
fabric of the canopies above
the four-poster beds.

CANOPIES

Left. On Saint-Barthélemy in the West Indies, a Swedish woman fell head over heels in love with this superb colonial house, which she rescued from its neglected state. In her bedroom, there is a majestic four-poster bed beneath a diaphanous mosquito net. Delicate, Swiss cotton curtains filter the bright light from outside. Just a few pieces of wooden furniture and white hangings make up the decor. The result is a bedroom that is at once austere and feminine.

Right. Adeline Dieudonné, who runs the Noël linen company, has chosen to embellish this wood and straw bed with simple, white cotton linen that is embroidered with a verdure lattice pattern and enhanced by a mohair blanket. A small cushion, with salient-lined borders, matches the green motifs.

CANOPIES

Above. In Rajasthan, near Jaipur in India, stands a majestic Moghul-style fort that has been turned into a sublime hotel. There, some bedrooms have been installed in the hotel garden beneath sumptuous traditional tents—replicas of those used by the maharajahs on their campaigns—which give the illusion of a huge, canopied four-poster bed. A hand-embroidered cotton fabric covers the interior of this tent. The counterpane on the bed comes from the State of Gujurat. The furniture also mimicks that used by the maharajahs. The prints are reproductions of leading figures from Jaipur and Udaipur.

Above. In her Paris apartment near the Bastille, Corinne Fossey mixes styles and periods with wit and imagination. This four-poster bed, designed by Philippe Renaud and Patrice Gruffaz, is an allusion to the frivolous and rustic 18th century. It was made with rough planks painted white and rods of ferro-cement. It is covered with heavy cotton displaying grape-bunch motifs. This decor is lightened by touches of bright color: curtains of yellow satin, which make the light "sparkle," and lampshades set like exclamation points on lamps made of twisted wire. It all culminates in a frivolous and sassy style.

CANOPIES

Left. The Begawan Giri, on
the island of Bali, is one of
the world's loveliest hotels.
Bradley and Debbie Gardner,
under the leadership of
architect Cheong Yew Kuan,
have designed a place that is
peerless. There is no showy
architecture, but rather a desire
to blend in as much as possible
with nature. This suite is
installed in a splendid house
opening onto a wide terrace.
Three large bamboo doors close
off the bathroom. The furniture
is simple, but the bathtub,
carved into a rock, lends
a little note of luxury.

Right. In the Seychelles,
on Frégate Island, the
decoration of this hotel
bedroom conjures up the
ambience of the South Seas
and Asia. Teak and mahogany,
art objects and antiques rub
shoulders with colonial style
furniture. A linen mosquito
net has been slung across
the four-poster bed. The result
is simple luxury beneath a roof
woven with ylang-ylang.

CANOPIES

Left. The Toiny Hotel, on the island of Saint-Barthélemy, consists of 13 independent bungalows with light-colored, well-lit bedrooms. All of the furniture in this room is made of solid mahogany—inspired by the furniture once found in the homes of planters on Martinique. The ceiling is made of varnished wood. On the four-poster bed, a small quilt in cotton piqué, and lined with toile de Jouy, lends a note of comfort.

Right. Vanna Bellazzi, a film and advertising set designer, has chosen to make her home in Milan. With her friend, architect Roberto Gerosa, she has designed this bedroom in a spare, monastic style. It is the only room in the house with a door to shut it off from the rest of the living space. The wooden bed was designed by Mauro Mori. Light silk tumbles from its pillars. The copper and paper lamp, set on a 17th century painted wood desk, was made by Roberto Gerosa.

Left. For André and Françoise Lafon's home near Marrakesh, in Morocco, Françoise handled the interior decoration. In her bedroom, around the traditional brass bed, she has arranged objects that were bargain-hunted in antique stores and found in flea markets.
Above. Still in Marrakesh, in the property of Quito Fiero, interior decorator Jacqueline Foissac shrewdly mixes Art Deco and Oriental hues.

CANOPIES

Irène and Giorgio Silvagni,
celebrities in the fashion
and film world, fell in love
with a house in Provence.
As the months passed, they
turned their Provençal
farmhouse into an amazing
abode, by using colorful
and unconventional decoration.
For their daughter's bedroom,
they chose a Klein blue,
conjuring up Matisse. It was
Giorgio himself who created
the color by mixing the desired
pigments. He also made the
four-poster bed using recycled
materials (wooden planks,
furniture legs, etc.).
These clever and inventive
creations give the room
an unconventional and
fanciful charm.

DRESSING ROOMS

BEAUTIFUL AND ELEGANT, IN SYCAMORE, MAHOGANY, CHESTNUT OR LEBANESE CEDAR, DRESSING ROOMS HAVE BECOME FULL-FLEDGED ROOMS IN THEIR OWN RIGHT. THE BEST OF THE BEST SHOW DESIGN SAVVY FOR STORAGE SPACES THAT ARE, IN A WORD, RATIONAL.

Left. This dressing room, in the home of furniture designer Philippe Hurel and wife Patricia, runs the length of a wall, like a library. The structure and drawers are in sycamore, and, thanks to a system of glass doors, you can decide at first glance what you will wear that day.

Above. In this room with cut-off corners that open onto the bedroom and bathroom, Baron and Baroness Reille have created a wonderful dressing room in solid oak. On the left, his corner, on the right, hers.

Above, left. In Donatella Versace's home, a large closet in mahogany and chestnut is devoted to storage space for her clothes. A full closet has been designed for her shoe collection.

Above, right. The dressing room of interior decorator Patrice Nourrissat has been designed in peeled deal, with a "lemon-tree"-colored stain, and varnished. It is divided into different storage areas. The shoes fill a narrow cupboard.

Right. His area has been arranged so that he can choose boxers and shoes at a glance.

DRESSING ROOMS

Opposite, top. Patrice Nourrissat's huge dressing room offers an overall view of the wardrobe, shown in its best light. On the fir ceiling, gray-tinted diagonals have been drawn.

Opposite, bottom. The hanging space for jackets has been designed on two levels.

Right. As for his shirts, these are arranged in Plexiglas drawers

DRESSING ROOMS

Left. Architects Daniel and
Michel Bismut have come up
with a superb interior design,
which is both contemporary
and classic, for this new
building in Boulogne, northern
France. A bedroom connects to
this striking dressing room-
cum-library made of stained
mahogany, with bronze knobs
and handles. It forms a narrow
room, where hanging space,
shelving, drawers and books
have all been accommodated.

Right. Federica, an interior
decorator in Geneva—where
she runs the Interiors store—
has set up home in a chalet
above Gstaad. Her chalet
doesn't really conform to
traditional Alpine style,
but rather opts for simplicity
and practicality. An example
of this is evident in this
dressing room with its
spacious compartments
and large drawers.

DRESSING ROOMS

On the wooded heights above
Geneva, architect Rémi Tessier
has designed a discreetly
luxurious home. The chic, yet
functional, dressing room is
made entirely of Lebanese
cedar, a moth-repellent wood.
He has shrewdly fitted in many
wardrobes, drawers and shelves.
The door is a moucharabieh,
which creates a lovely effect
of filtered light. The chair is a
Jean-Michel Frank design.

Left. Architects Daniel and Michel Bismut have redesigned the spaces of a townhouse in Neuilly, near Paris. For the dressing room, they have chosen precious wood: bleached sycamore. It is framed by strips of wenge, as is the mirror. A Hermès "whitebus" shopping bag sits on the chair. **Above.** This dressing room in painted wood and MDF, was designed by Christian Liaigre for the owner of a duplex in La Madeleine neighborhood in Paris. It reflects a spare, almost monastic decoration, based essentially on natural components in neutral colors, and results in harmonious and effective simplicity.

Left. Designed by interior decorator Yves Taralon, this unisex dressing room is in mahogany with an interplay of mirrors, here and there, to make the room seem bigger and give it greater clarity. A blind in the same wood covers the window. The patterns on the armchair and rug go perfectly with the warm hue of the wood.

Opposite. Thanks to architect Paola Piva, who designed this kit dressing room in solid walnut, you can put together endless varied arrangements by adapting them to their surroundings and, needless to say, to what graces your wardrobe. The drawers have leather or wood facings, the pull-out handles are made of brass, and the sock drawers divide into compartments with four partitions.

Left. In Patrice Nourrissat's
spacious dressing room,
a splendid chest in peeled fir,
with many different-sized
drawers, has been specially
designed for keeping small
clothing items—like his
socks, which appear in a
rainbow of colors.

Right. Patrice Nourrissat
also created this tall piece of
furniture made of see-through
Perspex, for keeping his shirts.
Overlooking a delightful interior
garden, the windows are veiled
by wood-slatted blinds.

DRESSING ROOMS

Opposite. The clever and
ingenious system that Patrice
Nourrissat has come up with
for keeping his shirts:
Plexiglas drawers, one on
top of the other.

Right. The dressing room of a
Parisian architect illustrates
a very orderly way of keeping
shirts, since each drawer can
hold just two. Another
interesting detail worth noting:
the hanging rail for the suits
can be tipped by a long
handle that pulls it downward.

DRESSING ROOMS

Patrick Frèche and his
family have been living in
a five-floor 1930s'-style house
in Paris since 1983. The fourth
floor accommodates a bedroom
and a sublime dressing room
made of solid mahogany.
The room and its many storage
compartments are perfectly
lit by small, adjustable low-watt
lights. With the exception of the
shirts and suits, the clothes
have been designed by Patrick
for his Loft fashion stores.

ALCOVES

IN THE 17TH CENTURY, THE SPANISH WORD ALCOVE MEANT A "LITTLE BED-
ROOM." THERE, LADIES OF POLITE SOCIETY, KNOWN AS "PRÉCIEUSES,"
WOULD RECEIVE THEIR GUESTS AND HOLD SALONS. THESE DAYS, BEDS
NESTLING IN ALCOVES GIVE THE IMPRESSION OF COZY COMFORT.

Left. In this bedroom, with its Le Manach printed wallpaper, the headboard fits snugly into an alcove adorned with an 18th century architectural drawing. The mahogany bedside table was designed by Alain Raynaud.

The sheets and pillowcases are the work of Christian Benais. **Above.** In his 19th century apartment in Paris, Christian Benais has installed this decor—which was created for the 1991 launching of the Chanel perfume, Egoïste.

A very neo-classical style was
evident in Bill Blass' New York
City apartment. The couturier
chose neutral tones for the
walls, which contrast with
the mahogany parquet and
the paisley pattern of the bed
linen. In the middle of the
room, the large mahogany
pedestal table from the Empire
period acts as a stand for an old
reproduction of the Vendôme
column. On the right, he had
an equestrian bronze of
Napoléon. This room exudes
a very masculine taste,
of neo-Palladian inspiration.

Above. Zurich hairdresser Rudolf Haene designed this bed for the guest room in his Swiss chalet. The bed was then made by a local craftsman.

The wood decor, combined with the whiteness of the linens and hangings, creates a pleasant feeling of comfort.

Above. In this bedroom of Anglo-Indian inspiration— where the bed is tucked into an alcove—cupboards with small shutter doors act as wardrobes.

A Bertoïa bench has been placed at the foot of the bed— which is covered with white, antique linen sheets and a printed silk bedspread.

ALCOVES

Top, left.
At Le Chaufourg, a Périgord guest house, this room is lit by two French windows and, above all, by this unusually large bull's-eye window. The rounded, wooden moldings are painted white and conceal large wardrobes. The bedside tables were specially designed and made by a local blacksmith. The cane bench is Napoléon III.

Top, right.
Still at Le Chaufourg, two family portraits hang on the ocher walls, which feature brushed and waxed rendered finish. The bed fits in an alcove where the dominant feature is a piece of Louis XVI woodwork. The floor has been created with different types of old terra cotta tiles.

Bottom, left.
The two oak sofas in the ante-room can be used as beds, if need be. They were designed by Anthony Collett and Andrew Zarzycki, as was the hazelwood bed. The carpet is a dhurrie purchased in London and cut to size.

Bottom, right.
On the Berber bed, an old, Provençal quilted bedspread and white linen. The walls are covered with tadlakt.

ALCOVES

In the bedroom of Swiss
hairdresser Rudolf Haene,
a canopy bed covered in
linens displays a pleasing mix
of blue patterns. Brass
wall lights have been screwed
to the bed's uprights. A carved,
wooden cuckoo clock adds
a touch of nostalgia.

HEADBOARDS

MATERIALS, COLORS, PATTERNS: HEADBOARDS MAKE ALL MANNER OF WHIM AND FANCY POSSIBLE, AND CAN BE STRUCTURED LIKE ACTUAL SCREENS OR PARTITIONS. THEY CUNNINGLY ROUND OFF THE DECORATION OF A BEDROOM, AND LEND A TOUCH OF COMFORT AT THE SAME TIME.

Left. This headboard features vivid colors. The sheets and pillowcases are by Michèle Halard for Puymorin, and the yellow cushion comes from Porthault. The bedspread is by Portobello. The wooden surface comes from the Conran Shop, and the framed poster on the wall is from the Pompidou Center museum in Paris.

Above. In this room, the headboard, bedside table and bench table, all in ebony, were designed by architect Rémi Tessier. Muriel Grateau created the linen, and the reading lights were designed and made by Manufactor.

Chic sobriety wins out in this
bedroom, where the screen
acting as a headboard can also
be used to hide storage units.
Made of fir wood, it is the kind
you can assemble yourself.

Left. A very relaxed kind of refinement is revealed in this bedroom, which juggles with the contrasts between dark wood and light paint. The ash wood shelves for objects and books were designed by Catherine Memmi, as were the linen sheets and Merino wool blanket. The curtains are made of silk lined with wool and angora.

Above. This headboard in Frédéric Méchiche's home is enlivened by the stripes he is so fond of. On the wall, a painting by Jean-Claude Blais is lit by a string of fairy lights. A 19th century plaster cast vase sits on the right.

HEADBOARDS

To furnish this picture-free
bedroom, Didier Gomez
had the idea of putting a
huge screen against the
rear wall. The screen, like the
bedside tables, is made of cedar.
At the foot of the bed rests a
bench designed by Didier for
putting books and clothes on.
The room also features an
armchair and a daybed.

Above. A gentle and airy atmosphere predominates in this two-tone bedroom. Interior designer Axel Verhoustraeten has gone for contrasts—with the floor, dressing room and radiator cover top, all made of wenge, strikingly setting off the ecru-colored bed, and the chaise longue by Christian Liaigre. **Right.** Edith Mézard's version of a bed is one on which you can work by day. To keep it thoroughly clean, she has added to the top sheet a width of linen which partly covers the sheet's turned-down border. The pillows have two-tone linen pillowcases that match the covers, and the headboard is covered with the same linen.

Above. In decorator Michèle Rédélé's chalet bedroom, the walls and headboard are made of "windfall" wood that has been whitewashed. The uprights and moldings are in old wood. The tapestry curtains and the net curtains are hung on hammered steel curtain rods.

Right. This small Provençal bedroom features a thoroughly simple headboard. The neutral quality of the taupe hue of the walls is enhanced by the bright shades of the sheets. The zinc lamp was designed by Yves Halard.

Above. A 19th century Chinese screen brings an Oriental atmosphere to this house in Flanders, decorated by Lionel Jadot. A mixture of silk and velvet was used for the cushions, and velveteen for the studded headboard from Vanhamme. The four spiral bed posts are connected to one another by lengths of bamboo. **Right.** A sober, clean design is present in this bedroom that plays with natural colors. Over the headboard, decorator Henri Becq has put a striking sculpture by Raphaël Scorbiac entitled *Twenty-one People Waiting for Happiness.* On each side of the sycamore bed—stained the color of rosewood—two stools in stained ash wood serve as bedside tables.

Above. Architect Laurent Bourgois has chosen a headboard covered with fabric to add to his soft and comfy room. Wall lights cast their glow over the bedside tables by Christian Liaigre.
Right. This beautiful suzani.

used as a bedspread, inspired Françoise Dorget—founder of the Caravane store in Paris—to use colors matching the embroideries for the sheets and pillowcases. The dark plum-colored shade has also been used for the velvet headboard to

create a contrast with the daintiness of the bedspread. To top it off, she has hung a rush mat with grayish-brown and plum-colored stripes. The bed is lit by two bamboo lamps, their shades covered with a fabric made of manilla hemp and silk.

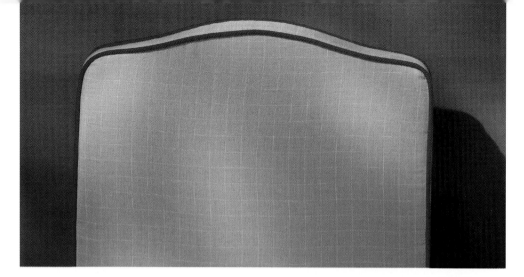

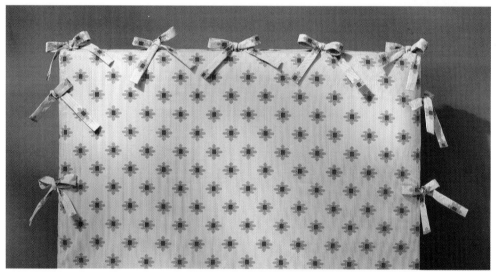

To make a headboard cover, you must allow for almost an inch of extra fabric around each cutout piece, for the stitching. The cover is always open at the bottom. **Top.** Duvivier headboard. "Pondicherry" linen fabric, Design Guild. **Bottom.** Renault headboard, "Aix" cotton fabric, Comoglio. **Right, from back to front.** Louis XVI classicism in this Merinos headboard in "Alizée" cotton fabric from Urgé. A country feel with this headboard, "Escoussetto" cotton by Les Olivades. Absolute simplicity: this headboard is in 100% "Raies" cotton fabric by Les Impressions.

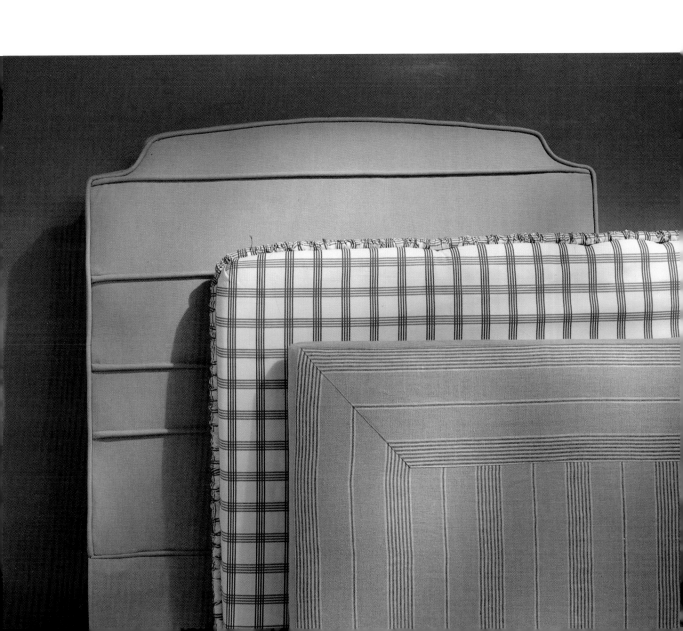

Left, top. The patterns on this headboard—made in white flannel on gray flannel— were inspired by an 8th century Scandinavian stela. The sheets and pillowcases are by Inès de La Fressange.

Left, bottom. This imaginative headboard with rosettes in staggered rows is in 100% "Sorgues" cotton fabric by Pierre Frey.

Right. A simple geometry and bright colors predominates in this contemporary style headboard. The "Salzbourg" fabric is by Nobilis. The brown, blue and red "Samourai" braid is by Houlès. Sheets and pillowcases are by Puymorin. A Hermès plaid and a Souléiado bedspread are the final touch. Yves Halard designed the bedside tables and cups.

Useful Addresses

FURNITURE AND ACCESSORIES

ABC CARPET
(ARTIFACTS, FURNITURE)
www.abchome.com
P: 212-473-3000

B & B ITALIA
(BEDS, STORAGE UNITS, WARDROBES)
www.bebitalia.it
P: 800-872-1697

BAKER FURNITURE
(CHAIRS)
www.bakerfurniture.com
P: 800-59-BAKER

BRITISH KHAKI
(HANDCRAFTED FURNITURE)
www.britishkhaki.com
P: 212-343-2299

CASSINA
(BEDS, CHAIRS, STORAGE UNITS)
www.cassinausa.com
P: 800-770-3568

CENTURY
(TRADITIONAL FURNITURE)
www.centuryfurniture.com
P: 800-852-5552

CHARLES P. ROGERS
(BEDS)
www.charlesprogers.com
P: 800-561-0467

CRATE & BARREL
(ACCESSORIES, BEDS, LINENS)
www.crateandbarrel.com
P: 800-967-6696

DENNIS MILLER ASSOCIATES
(DESIGN CHAIRS, LOUNGE, TABLES)
www.dennismiller.com
P: 212-684-0070

FLOU
(BEDS, BED ACCESSORIES)
www.flou.com

HENREDON
(FURNITURE, UPHOLSTERY)
www.henredon.com
P: 800-444-3682

HERMAN MILLER
(ARMCHAIRS, END TABLES)
www.hermanmiller.com
P: 888-443-4357

HICKORY CHAIR
(TRADITIONAL FURNITURE)
www.hickorychair.com
P: 828-324-1801

IKEA
(ACCESSORIES, FURNITURE)
www.ikea-usa.com

KNOLL
(DESIGN CHAIRS, DESKS, TABLES)
www.knoll.com
P: 800-343-5665

LAFCO
(ACCESSORIES, FURNITURE, WARDROBES)
www.lafcony.com
P: 800-362-3677

LES MIGRATEURS
(FURNITURE, UPHOLSTERY)
www.lesmigrateurs.com
P: 207-846-1430

OLY
(ACCESSOIRES, FURNITURE)
www.olystudio.com
P: 510-644-1870

PIER 1 IMPORTS
(ACCESSORIES, FURNITURE,
LINENS)
www.pier1.com
P: 800-245-4595

POLIFORM USA
(CONTEMPORARY FURNITURE)
www.poliformusa.com
P: 888-POLIFORM

POTTERY BARN
(ACCESSORIES, FURNITURE,
LINENS)
www.potterybarn.com
P: 888-779-5176

PUCCI
(CONTEMPORARY FURNITURE)
www.ralphpucci.com
P: 212-633-0452

REPERTOIRE
(FURNITURE)
www.repertoire.com
P: 212-219-8159

RESTORATION HARDWARE
(ACCESSORIES, FURNITURE)
www.restorationhardware.com
P: 800-762-1005

ROCHE BOBOIS
(CONTEMPORARY FURNITURE)
www.roche-bobois.com
P: 800-972-8375

STOREHOUSE
(FURNITURE)
www.storehouse.com
P: 888-STOREHOUSE

LINENS

ANICHINI
(ACCESSORIES, LINENS)
www.anichini.com
P: 800-553-5309

**BONJOUR OF
SWITZERLAND**
(LINENS)
www.bonswit.com
P: 877-BONSWIT

CALVIN KLEIN
(ACCESSORIES, LINENS)
P: 800-294-7978
(store locations)

CHAMBERS
(ACCESSORIES, LINENS)
P: 800-334-9790

COULEUR NATURE
(HAND-STICHED QUILTS,
LINENS)
www.couleurnature.com
P: 866-623-6826

FIELDCREST CANNON
(LINENS)
www.charismahome.com
P: 800-841-3336

FRETTE
(ACCESSORIES, LINENS)
www.frette.com
P: 800-35-FRETTE

GARNET HILL
(HOME FURNISHINGS,
LINENS)
www.garnethill.com
P: 800-622-6216

MATTEO
(ACCESSORIES, LINENS)
www.matteohome.com
P: 888-MATTEO-1

NANCY KOLTES
(ACCESSORIES, LINENS)
www.nancykoltes.com

NAUTICA
(LINENS)
www.nautica.com
P: 877-NAUTICA

PEACOCK ALLEY
(LINENS)
www.peacockalley.com
P: 800-810-0708

PINECONE HILL
(ACCESSORIES, LINENS)
www.pineconehill.com
P: 413-496-9700

PORTHAULT
(ACCESSORIES, LINENS)
www.dporthault.fr
P: 212-688-1660

PRATESI
(ACCESSORIES, LINENS)
www.pratesi.com
P: 800-332-6925

RALPH LAUREN
(ACCESSORIES, LINENS,
TEXTILES)
www.rlhome.polo.com
P: 888-475-7674

SFERRA BROS
(LINENS)
www.sferrabros.com
P: 800-336-1891

SUE FISHER KING
(HOME FURNISHINGS,
LINENS)
www.suefisherking.com
P: 888-811-7276

WAMSUTTA/SPRINGS
(LINENS)
www.springs.com
P: 888-WAMSUTTA

WEST ELM
(ACCESSORIES, LINENS,
HOME FURNISHINGS)
www.westelm.com
P: 866-428-6468

WESTPOINT STEVENS
(LINENS)
www.westpointstevens.com
P: 800-533-8229

FABRICS AND RUGS

ABC CARPET
(LUXURY CARPETS, FABRICS)
www.abchome.com
P: 212-473-3000

BERGAMO
(LUXURY FABRICS)
www.bergamofabrics.com
P: 914-665-0800

BOUSSAC
(ACCESSORIES, LUXURY
FABRICS)
www.boussac-fadini.fr
P: 866-268-7722

BRUNSCHWIG & FILS
(FABRICS, HOME
FURNISHINGS, LAMPS)
www.brunschwig.com

CAPEL
(AREA RUGS)
www.capelrugs.com
P: 800-382-6574

COURISTAN
(RUGS)
www.couristan.com
P: 800-223-6186

EDELMAN LEATHER
(LEATHER SPECIALISTS)
www.edelmanleather.com
P: 800-886-8339

F. SCHUMACHER & CO.
(HOME FASHIONS, FABRICS,
WALLPAPER)
www.fschumacher.com
P: 800-332-3384

HABIDECOR
(LUXURY RUGS)
www.habidecorusa.com
P: 800-588-8565

J. ROBERT SCOTT
(ACCESSORIES, HOME
FURNISHINGS, TEXTILES)
www.jrobertscott.com
P: 800-322-4910

KRAVET
(FABRICS, TRIMMINGS)
www.kravet.com
P: 800-648-KRAV

ODEGARD
(LUXURY CARPETS)
www.odegardinc.com
P: 800-670-8836

WAVERLY
(FABRICS, WALLPAPER)
www.waverly.com
P: 800-423-5881

LIGHTING

ROBERT ABBEY
(LIGHTING DESIGN)
www.robertabbey.com
P: 828-322-3480

CX DESIGN
(LAMPS)
P: 888-431-4242

FLOS
(LIGHTING DESIGN)
www.flos.net
P: 800-939-3567

NAMBE
(ACCESSORIES, LIGHTING
DESIGN)
www.nambe.com
P: 800-443-0339

JAMIE YOUNG
(ACCESSORIES, LIGHTING
DESIGN)
www.jamieyoung.com
P: 888-671-5883

BEDDING

**PACIFIC COAST
FEATHER CO.**
(COMFORTERS, FEATHERBEDS)
www.pacificcoast.com
P: 888-297-1778

SEALY
(MATTRESSES)
www.sealy.com
P: 800-MY-SEALY

SERTA
(MATTRESSES)
www.serta.com
P: 888-557-3782

UNITED FEATHER & DOWN
(DOWN, FEATHER PRODUCTS)
www.ufandd.com
P: 847-296-6500

Photographs by:

Guillaume de Laubier: pp. 10, 11, 16-17, 24-25, 30-31, 32, 33, 36-37, 41, 42, 44, 45, 56, 57, 59, 65, 70 to 76, 81, 82, 84, 86, 87, 95, 96 (top and bottom), 97 (top), 104, 108, 109, 112, 115

Marianne Haas: pp. 8, 9, 15, 26-27, 28, 29, 46 to 49, 52, 53, 66 to 69, 77 to 80, 83, 90, 92-93, 97(bottom), 101, 110

Didier Massard: pp. 100, 116 (top and bottom), 117, 118 (top and bottom), 119

Jacques Dirand: pp. 12-13, 14, 18, 39, 55, 61, 64, 105, 106-107

Gilles de Chabaneix: pp. 19, 34, 35, 45, 54, 88-89

Alexandre Bailhache: pp. 50-51, 91

Patrice Pascal: pp. 102-103, 114

Reto Güntli: pp. 94, 98-99

Édouard Sicot: pp. 23, 40

Fritz von den Schulenburg/Inside: pp. 20, 21

Gilles Trillard: pp. 22, 111

Vera Cruz: p. 38

Guy Bouchet: p. 43

Antoine Rozès: p. 58

Pierre-Olivier Deschamps/Vu: p. 60

Philippe Costes: p. 62

Deidi von Schaewen: p. 63

Pascal Himous/Top: p. 85

Séline Keller: p. 113

Words by:

Marie-Claire Blanckaert: pp. 8, 9, 10, 11, 12-13, 15 to 18, 22 to 33, 36 to 39, 41 to 44, 45, 46 to 49, 53 to 57, 59, 60, 63, 65 to 76, 78 to 89, 94 to 99, 101 to 113, 115

Barbara Bourgois: pp. 35, 100, 114, 116 (top and bottom), 117, 118 (bottom), 119

Marie Kalt: pp. 14, 50-51, 61, 64

Paul-Marie Sorel: pp. 34, 52

Alexandra d'Arnoux: pp. 58, 90

François Baudot: p. 92-93

Catherine Scotto: p. 62

Philippe Seulliet: p. 77.

Marie-Claude Dumoulin: p.19

Françoise Tournier: p. 118 (haut)

Elle Decor (U.S.) and *Elle Décoration* (France) are both imprints of the Hachette Filipacchi group.
The content of this book was taken solely from *Elle Décoration* and appeared only in France.

WE WOULD LIKE TO THANK THE OWNERS, DECORATORS, INSTITUTIONS OR HOTELS THAT HAVE WELCOMED *ELLE DECOR* COLLABORATORS FOR THEIR REPORTAGES:

MEHMET BAY, HENRI BECQ, MICHÈLE AND PAUL BELAICHE, VANNA BELLAZZI, CHRISTIAN BENAIS, DANIEL AND MICHEL BISMUT, BILL BLASS, MARC BLONDEAU, LAURENT BOURGOIS, DAVID CHAMPION, JEAN-ANDRÉ AND GENEVIÈVE CHARRIAL, CHÂTEAU DE BAGNOLS (PAUL AND HÉLÈNE HAMLYN, BEAUJOLAIS), LE CHAUFOURG (GEORGES DAMBIER, PÉRIGORD), ANTHONY COLLETT, AGNÈS COMAR, ADELINE DIEUDONNÉ, FRANÇOISE DORGET, QUITO FIERO, JACQUELINE FOISSAC, CORINNE FOSSEY, PATRICK FRÈCHE, ZEYNEP GARAN, ROBERTO GEROSA, DIDIER GOMEZ, JEAN AND TERRY DE GUNZBURG, RUDOLF HAENE, ANOUSKA HEMPEL, HÔTEL ALBERT I (LUXEMBOURG), BEGAWAN GIRI HOTEL (BRADLEY AND DEBBIE GARDNER, BALI), BLAKES HOTEL (AMSTERDAM), FRÉGATE ISLAND HOTEL (SEYCHELLES), HEMPEL HOTEL (LONDON), DOKHAN'S HOTEL (PARIS), HÔTEL LE TOINY (GUADELOUPE), RAJVILAS HOTEL (JAIPUR, INDIA), ROSHEIM HOTEL (NORWAY), TERRY HUNZIKER, PHILIPPE AND PATRICIA HUREL, JEAN-CLAUDE JACQUEMART, LIONEL JADOT, MAXIME DE LA FALAISE, FRANÇOISE AND ANDRÉ LAFON, JACQUES LEGUENNEC, JACKY LORENZETTI, JOHN MAC LEOD, FRANÇOIS MARCQ, FRÉDÉRIC MÉCHICHE, CATHERINE MEMMI, ÉDITH MÉZARD, MONIQUE AND LAURENT NORMAND, PATRICE NOURRISSAT, RÉGIS PAGNEZ, FEDERICA AND LUIS PALACIOS, DANIEL AND OLIVIER PELENC, PAOLO PIVA, JULIE PRISCA, ALAIN RAYNAUD, MICHÈLE RÉDÉLÉ, BARON AND BARONESS REILLE, SARAH SAINT-GEORGES, CHRISTIAN SAPET, BRIGITTE SEMTOB, IRÈNE AND GIORGIO SILVAGNI, YVES TARALON, RÉMI TESSIER, AUDE DE THUIN, DAVID TIGER, AXEL VERHOUSTRAETEN, DONATELLA VERSACE.

**Under the direction of
Jean Demachy**

Editorial
Marie-Claire Blanckaert

Art Direction
Anne-Marie Chéret

Editing
Nicolas Rabeau

Photo research
Geneviève Tartrat

Text research
Sandrine Hess